Spirit of the Kitchen

Spirit of the Kitchen

Jane Alexander

For Adrian, the kitchen god—and all who

share our table

Element
An Imprint of HarperCollins*Publishers*
77–85 Fulham Palace Road,
Hammersmith, London W6 8JB

The Element website is: www. elementbooks.co.uk

Published by Element 2002

10 9 8 7 6 5 4 3 2 1

Text copyright © Jane Alexander 2002
Copyright © HarperCollins*Publishers* Ltd 2002
Jacket image © Tim Goffe

Jane Alexander asserts the moral right
to be identified as the author of this work

Editor: Jillian Stewart
Design: Wheelhouse Creative
Production: Melanie Vandevelde
Photography: see page 90 for credits

A catalogue record for this book
is available from the British Library

ISBN 0 00 713677 3

Printed and bound in Hong Kong

Contents

Introduction

What is a kitchen? It sounds like a simple question but when you think about it, of all the rooms in the house, the image of the "kitchen" is perhaps the most protean; it shimmies and slides like a lively fish. A kitchen is a place for preparing and cooking food—that is a given. But that food can be lovingly prepared and transformed into culinary alchemy—or it can be thrown into a microwave, zapped with rays, and then slung on a plate. A kitchen can be a place where the cook holds a solitary reign, either happy in his or her splendid chef-like isolation or miserable in banishment, enslaved by the cooker and the appetites of a demanding family. Or a kitchen can be the hub of the house; a lively place of discussion and debate; a gathering place for family and friends; a sociable space.

It's interesting that, over the last fifty years or so, the kitchen has become elevated in stature and prestige. In the past, kitchen "design" as such barely existed. Furniture and fittings were utilitarian: people didn't really think about the kitchen as a space to be designed and decorated. As the age of science took over, inventions started to make domestic life easier. Machinery took the toil out of housework—and nowhere more than in the kitchen. Of all the rooms in the house, your kitchen is most likely the one with the battery of machines: fridges, freezers, washing machines and dryers, dishwashers, ovens, stoves, grills, microwaves. Not to mention the vast array of gadgets and specialist equipment: bread makers, ice-cream makers, waffle makers, toasters, food processors. On the other hand, a wider knowledge of the danger of germs in the cooking process led to a fascination, almost obsession, with hygiene. Maybe it was this invasion of science and hygiene into the kitchen that prompted a move toward more clinical design. The kitchen mutated from a homely, haphazard room into a laboratory of food.

Nowadays a new kitchen can cost as much as a small house. "Designer" kitchens come in a bewildering array of styles and colors and the "new kitchen" is a definite status symbol. Why? My feeling is that we are trying, desperately, to rekindle the heart of our homes. In this hurried, hassled world, we have lost our connection with our sense of center and also with the Earth, our Mother, and this fracture leaves us with a chill, lonely feeling in the heart. Somewhere, deep inside, we have the knowledge that we can rediscover this link, if not in the fields and forests, then in a small way in our kitchens (and, incidentally, in our gardens—another boom area). So we have deified the art of cookery, turned chefs into TV celebrities, transformed our kitchens into high-tech, high-cost temples of hygiene and efficiency. We hopefully pray that, if we follow the recipes of our new-found domestic gods and goddesses to the letter, we will rediscover our sense of belonging. Sadly, it doesn't happen.

We need to reclaim the real heart of the kitchen and turn it into the living, breathing center of our homes. It's interesting that many people are now combining kitchens and living rooms into one open-plan "living area." At an unconscious level, we're seeking to integrate our psyches with our homes. We're looking for a way of finding the hearth once again (more on this in the next chapter).

I'm writing this book almost in tandem with another in the series, *Spirit of the Living Room*, because they share many concepts. If your kitchen is tiny, you will automatically need to transfer some of its duties onto the living room. If you don't have a living hearth in your living room, you will have to honor Hestia, goddess of the hearth, in your kitchen. This isn't some cunning marketing ploy, but I'd suggest you read the two books together if you want to feel the total overlap of these domestic spaces.

My own kitchen is a madcap space. We inherited a gloomy north-facing kitchen, peopled with pretty ghastly wood-effect units and absolutely disgusting tiles. The previous owners had split the room in two and routed a staircase through part of it, so you had to duck to sit down at the table. The only redeeming feature was a bright-red oven-stove (more on AGA in the "Practical Kitchen" chapter). Monty, the boxer dog, immediately decided this was his long-lost twin and set up permanent residence in front of it. Our budget was virtually zero but we realized that if we wanted any kind of domestic calm in this house we needed a fully functioning kitchen. So down came the connecting walls and the staircase and immediately we had a much larger working space. We couldn't afford to buy new units or tiles so we painted them white to reflect some light. Looking outside on a fresh spring morning I noticed the color of the brand-new beech leaves and decided this had to be the color for our kitchen—pulling in the spirit of outdoors and the wild. Our old scrub-top pine table fitted in just fine and provides a good place for family and friends to sit and talk (or interfere) as Adrian, my husband the super-cook, prepares food. We battle furiously with clutter and I confess our tabletop is rarely clear but tends to accumulate papers, books, bills, and a fair sprinkling of toys. Since the arrival of James, our son, the kitchen also serves variously as playroom and artist's studio (James's easel stands ever-ready in a corner waiting for inspiration to strike). His daubings also decorate the large food cupboard.

Our kitchen is a noisy place. We don't have a utility room so the washing machine usually provides a background hum (or thud). We like music in the kitchen so we gently battle over who gets to choose it. And, of course, we sit at the table for our meals and talk, debate, argue, laugh. When friends come around, we often don't make it as far as the living room and the formal dining table because we can't prise our guests away from the kitchen. But add a few candles, some aromatherapy oils, and a vase of flowers and the kitchen table is transformed.

Sometimes I fantasize about hand-crafted wood units. I certainly dream of a beautiful new floor. I would undoubtedly adore a huge colorful fridge. But I can live without them because the spirit of our kitchen is just fine and dandy as it is.

This is not a kitchen design book—if you need to debate the precise siting of an oven or discuss the relative merits of various kinds of microwaves, there are plenty of other books which will merrily engage with you. This book is more a musing on what a kitchen is—or should be. It's not prescriptive, and I hope it takes into account the physical and financial limits many people will have. Above all, I hope it makes you think about your kitchen space and tempts you to find ways to make it a more comforting, hospitable place for the soul.

What is a Kitchen?

A kitchen is far more than a practical room for cooking. It is the center of the home, the focus, the heart. In ancient days the heart of the home was around the hearth; everyone would gather around the cookfire for warmth, company and, of course, the comfort of food. It was a place where the inside and outside met. Within the ancient kitchen, the woman of the house usually held court. It was a place of feminine nurturing and sustenance, the province of the Earth and Mother Goddesses. To enter the kitchen was to cross into a harbor of warmth and comfort. It's not surprising that many of the ancient symbols for the Mother Goddess are linked with cooking—the oven, the pot, the cooking vessel. But her symbols also include the magic circle and the mandala—spiritual glyphs of wholeness, togetherness, safety. Walking into the kitchen was like walking into a sanctuary, a place of safety and magic, in which both culinary and psychological alchemy took place.

In the archetypal kitchen, the "outside" would come in as other members of the family straggled in for food, warmth, and a good gossip. News of the external world would be discussed and chewed over around the hearth. Family fortunes and foreign disturbances would be food for thought.

Sadly, nowadays we rarely have this balance in our homes. Many homes no longer have a hearth, a living fire. So we look for that centering function from our kitchens, from our stoves, the symbolic flame. But what do we find? A clean, clinical laboratory for preparing food. A microwave instead of a heartening stove. A freezer stuffed with ready meals rather than nature's raw harvest. A television instead of a couple of cozy armchairs. Where are the herbs drying on the rack? Where are the jars of spices, pungent, sharp, and sweet? Where are the neat rows of pickles, preserves, and chutneys, awaiting the onset of winter? Instead of a well-thumbed journal of carefully handed-down recipes, we have piles of gleaming books full of flashy photography from celebrity chefs. Our kitchens have become status symbols—and we feel the lack.

In my earlier book *Spirit of the Home*, I lamented the loss of Hestia, goddess of the hearth, and suggested that we modern souls have embraced masculine archetypes such as Helios and Hermes at the expense of the more earthy goddesses of hearth, home, and nurturing. If you've read my earlier book, I apologize now—as I shall briefly recap why I think this denial is so unhealthy.

Helios (or Apollo) is the god of the sun, a masculine archetype that always seeks the light, the clear brightness, the sky. This archetype has ruled our consciousness for some considerable time as we seek to use science and the intellect to discover more about our world. It is the energy that likes to put

things "under the spotlight", to make "everything clear", that revels in fluorescent light under which no shadows lurk. It is the thrusting energy that has put a man on the moon and probes farther and farther into space. It is a necessary energy but, left unchecked, is a potentially dangerous one. When we seek only the sky, we neglect the earth. When we throw out our consciousness to embrace other planets and stars, we are withdrawing our attention from our own planet, our home. On a more personal level, we start to feel "spacey" and ungrounded—because we literally have forgotten the ground beneath us.

Unfortunately, the other leading archetype, Hermes (or Mercury) is equally spacey; in fact, we get a double dose of air, speed, and space. Hermes is the winged messenger of the gods, the expert communicator, who thrives on speed and intellect. Hermes, you could say, is the god of the telephone (or even better, the mobile phone), the fax, the computer (especially the laptop). He is the god of the media, of television and radio, newspapers and magazines; the Lord of the Internet. His currency is information, the more of it the better (you can bet your bottom dollar Hermes texts). His mode of transmission is quick, very quick. We have fallen in love with Hermes, with his swift agile mind; his restless, seeking nature; his charming, yet deceptive, trickster qualities. Hermes is the god of the fast buck, the conscience of the workaholic, the goad of the person who says more, just a little more. We all need Hermes in our lives, because without him existence can become very dull, but we are running the risk of toppling too far into his frenetic realm.

This may sound as if we're moving a long way from the kitchen sink—but, trust me, it is relevant. Fortunately there are natural antidotes to Helios' gleaming ambition and Hermes' frenetic information highway. Our kitchens were originally the home of two female archetypes, the goddesses Demeter (or Ceres) and Hestia (or Vesta). Demeter is the earth goddess, one of the many manifestations of the primal feminine form, the Great Mother. The Mother cherishes and sustains. She fosters growth, warmth, and intimacy; and is wise, loving, all-embracing. Her impulse is to gather people together, to nurture, to protect. As a corn goddess, Demeter was linked intrinsically with the most basic of foodstuffs—bread. She is the goddess of the cookpot, the original and vital domestic goddess. When we cook with care and love, we invoke Demeter.

When we shove a ready-meal in the microwave, we are throwing a nod to Hermes.

Hestia is the classical goddess of the hearth and home (and actually a form of the Mother in her own right). In Hestia we find the balance needed to offset Hermes' madness. He races around; she stays put. He looks for the new; she revels in the order of the known. He lures us out into the world, stretching ourselves further and further; she urges us back to the center, focusing on the deep, quiet needs of the soul.

Hestia resides in the kitchen; it is her natural domain. Unlike most Greek divinities, Hestia was very rarely represented in figurative form. She was understood to be present in the heart of every home, in the glowing embers of the household hearth. She was the fire at the center of the home, the spirit of the home, its organizing soul. Nowadays we don't gather around the central hearth—few of us have one. So Hestia has taken up her abode in the kitchen, around the warmth of the oven. No wonder we feel kitchens are so important to our lives.

Hestia imbues a house with spirit; her hearth offers the essential link with the earth. She also provides safety, security, and serenity. She brings together the people who live in a house—whether one or many—in an atmosphere of warmth and shelter.

She is a sociable goddess; she presided over the preparation of meals and the first mouthful of the meal was always consecrated to her. In Roman times "To Vesta" was a common grace. But although she can be seen, in one way, as the representative of Mother Earth, she is not a "mothering" goddess. Hestia always remained virgin, her own woman,

self-reliant and inward-looking. Her mood is one of quiet introspection and absorption, which is why she is such an obviously healthy balance when we have too much Hermetic energy whizzing around in our lives.

Demeter and Hestia have been overlooked and even ridiculed in the past fifty years as women sought and fought for their independence. However, I truly believe that we women should now have the confidence and sense of self-worth to be able to come back to the kitchen with joy. Can we be domestic goddesses? Absolutely, and it's vital soul work too. Many women desperately need to put themselves back in touch with their Hestia and Demeter values. They need to give themselves the time and space they crave for quiet reflection, for musing, for pottering, for stirring a pan, for dreaming over a stew pot.

It's not just an issue for women either. Nowadays men are realizing that they should explore and embrace their own feminine side, and getting into the kitchen can certainly help. However, so many men who embrace the kitchen do so in a totally Apollonian way. They make their cooking showy and flash; they miss the essential musing and internalizing which beckons Demeter and Hestia. My husband is an exception. When he cooks it is a sacred ritual. He lovingly chooses his ingredients, carefully picks his herbs, and crushes his spices. The sounds of classical music fill the air and he usually pours himself a libation of beer or wine to salute his own cooking gods and goddesses. Cooking is more than an art to him; it is a means of centering himself, of connecting with the earth and its bounty. Try as I might, I can't quite catch the peace and soulfulness with which he imbues his cooking—but I'm still trying. We'll look at this aspect of the kitchen again later.

For now, before we even start thinking about what we physically want in our kitchens, let's think about how we can start to put right the real basics. Let's think about how we can tempt Hestia back into the kitchen. Hestia is the one who makes space sacred, who demands that sometimes we close the doors and windows to the world and devote our time by focusing inward—on ourselves, our family, our home. She is the one who says "enough," who turns off the television and starts a conversation; who picks up a book instead of logging onto the web; who insists on shared family mealtimes rather than TV dinners. She is the one who can put tricky Hermes in his place. Interestingly, the Greeks understood perfectly the dynamic between Hermes and Hestia. While

Hestia governed the house itself, Hermes guarded the door, the threshold. He looked outward into the world; she focused inward. In some two-headed statues of door guardians there are representations, not of Janus, but of Hermes and Hestia. One looks out, the other looks in. They are in perfect balance. This is the model we need for our emotional health and well-being. We can't cut Hermes out altogether; that would be as unnatural as turning our backs on Hestia. We need communication, we need to let our minds expand outward as much as we need them to expand upward toward Helios, the sun. But just as we have to balance that upward striving with a remembrance of our earthly roots, we have to focus inward as well as out. Bringing Hestia back to her place in the heart of the house can start the healing process.

What do you want from your Kitchen?

Imagine your dream kitchen. Do you conjure a picture of a cozy, comfy farmhouse room, with worn flagstones on the floor, an old range with a kettle singing on top, and a scrub-top table with jars of wild flowers in the center? Or are you musing about a minimalist paean to high-tech, all gleaming white and chrome with industrial flooring and metal splashbacks? Do you see sunny Mediterranean colors—or neon pink or acid lime? Stop! At this stage it's too early to think about precise details like this—we need to muse a little on how we want our kitchens to feel and what functions they need to fulfill. Once we've discovered that, the practical bits will come far easier. Kitchens can be expensive rooms to fit and furnish, so it's well worth spending time working out what you really need.

Start noticing kitchens. Look at other people's—in fact, don't just look but feel, smell, and listen to them as well. Use all

your senses. How would you feel in such a kitchen? Would it work for you? Notice kitchens in magazines too and start cutting out pictures that appeal—not just whole kitchens but maybe colors or images that suggest the ideal mood of your kitchen. You can stick them in a journal or put them on a large sheet of paper as a kind of collage. Keep adding (and subtracting) from your image bank—you will probably find your ideas do change as you work through the processes in this book.

Kitchen memories

Often we unconsciously seek to recreate the atmosphere or physical reality of our own childhood spaces, particularly if an early kitchen is a potent and happy memory. Answer the following questions —either writing or painting your answers (or use a tape to record them). Note: if you had an unhappy childhood, you may find it safer to work through this with a trained counselor or psychotherapist.

- What is your earliest memory of the kitchen?
- Was your childhood kitchen/s a happy place/s? What incidents can you recall that happened in the kitchen?
- What scents, sounds, and feelings do you associate with your early kitchen/s?
- What are the first words that come to mind when you think about that room?
- What food did you eat as a child? What were your favorite, and most hated, meals?
- Who did the cooking in your home? Did they enjoy it or was it a chore?
- Did you sit down to eat as a family? Were mealtimes happy or tense?
- Did you help at all in the kitchen? What did you do and did you enjoy it?
- Are there any elements from that early kitchen that you would like to recreate in your own? Or do you think you're seeking the total opposite?

Allow yourself to muse, to dream, to go back in time and really remember. When I look back over the houses I have lived in, I realize that the most important element of the kitchen for me is always the big table. What stands out for you? Is there a mood, a feel, you would like to recreate? You may even fancy recreating the décor of those childhood kitchens: the utilitarian forties' kitchen; fifties' pastels, florals, and whimsical wallpapers; sixties' pop-art and geometric shapes; seventies' streamline furniture, coffee colors, and café art; eighties' chrome and high-tech, gleaming with gadgets. You don't need to follow the crowd, or the kitchen designers; a kitchen can be whatever you want it to be. If your favorite design is not "fashionable," there's nothing to stop you calling on the services of a local carpenter or cabinet maker to translate your desires—and it isn't any more expensive than buying most ready-made kitchen units.

Who uses your Kitchen?

The next important question to ask is "Who uses the kitchen?" and "What do they need from it?" We're told that every kitchen basically requires the same ingredients, and we buy into the belief that we all need long rows of cabinets and a triangle of oven, fridge, and sink. Not necessarily. Start by drawing a roughly-to-scale map of your kitchen space as it is. Put in all the various cabinets and appliances. Now color them in according to use. Pick a separate color for each person who uses the kitchen and shade in which bits they use (some will obviously become striped as several people will use them). It may be useful for everyone to do this exercise (as different people will have wildly different ideas of who uses what—and how much they use it). Certain areas may be completely oversubscribed; others may barely be used at all. What are in those cupboards or drawers which remained uncolored? Are they necessary? How could you make more space in the over-used areas? You may need to think about time-share schemes—the kids get certain hours for their homework, then the table is cleared for family dinner. After that, everyone takes a hand in clearing up so Mom can get out the laptop or Dad can write his novel.

If you have all come up with wildly differing views of who monopolizes the kitchen, then use your diagrams as a launching pad for a civilized discussion—allow everyone to have their say and try to figure out reasonable and fair compromises.

What's your type?

It may sound strange but the kind of kitchen your soul craves may be decided by your very personality. The psychologist Carl Jung believed that we can all be described by a system of four personality types and two modes of behavior. You're probably already familiar with the concept of extroverts and introverts: extroverts always reach out to the world, while introverts instinctively draw back from it. If you're an extrovert, you will probably care a lot how your home (and particularly your kitchen) is regarded by other people, as you undoubtedly entertain a lot and are highly sociable. If you're an introvert, you will be more concerned about what feels comfortable for you and you alone.

However, the process is more subtle than that. Jung realized that, aside from this basic division, people fell into four further categories, depending on how they approach life. Some deal with life by thinking; others by feeling; some rely on sensation (the information we receive through our senses); while others use intuition (information received directly from the subconscious). Each of us tends to use a mixture of two or perhaps three of these "functions," while there is usually one (or sometimes two) with which we don't identify. Let's see how this will apply to our ideal kitchens. You'll probably recognize yourself quite swiftly.

SENSATION: If you have a strong sensation function, you like things to work—and work well. You don't care if it's pretty as long as it gets the job done. A kitchen is there for cooking and practical chores and it needs to be perfectly ordered, with everything in its place. If a gadget doesn't do its job, out it goes. You're probably very "handy" around the house, great at do-it-yourself, and a firm believer in order. Every kitchen tool and implement will have its rightful place—and you will hate it if anyone interferes with your perfect plan.

INTUITION: You're less worried about how functional your kitchen may be than if the energy is flowing well. You're the kind of person who is naturally drawn to feng shui, space clearing, angels, and divinities. Practicality isn't really an issue—your kitchen needs to evoke a mood, a feeling. Yes, you cook in it, but a kitchen is far more to you: a temple, a retreat, a painting studio. You're probably wildly impractical yet incredibly inventive and artistic. Your kitchen will always invite comments.

THINKING: You probably never even think about your kitchen—unless a cupboard falls down or the cooker stops working. Thinking types are more concerned with ideas than things, and as long you have somewhere for your books (your kitchen probably has at least one bookcase if not more) you're usually happy. You don't give a fig for fads and fashions and so rarely even consider upgrading or redecorating.

FEELING: You notice everything in your kitchen—and you like it to look and feel right. It matters very much to you what color your kitchen is, how the units look, what the oven does, how your floor feels underfoot. You like your home to look and feel good to you and to others. You will go for comfort above all—but it needs to be fashionable comfort. Of all the types, you're the most likely to call in a professional designer, or to pore over design books yourself.

These key-note sketches should give you a good idea which function or functions you rely upon most heavily—they will also give you some valuable pointers. Let's look at what each type should watch out for:

• Sensation types might find it fun to loosen up a bit; to have some fun in their kitchens. Try opening yourself to the more esoteric ideas in this book, instead of swiftly turning the page. Have a go at space clearing, play with feng shui. Suspend disbelief. Although your ideal kitchen will undoubtedly be highly practical, you may find it far more fun if you allow a sense of play to come into your design.

• If you're a strong Intuitive, please make sure your kitchen is safe and just slightly practical. It's easy to forget to have the electrics and plumbing checked when you're so entranced with a design for a stained glass window.

You might get so carried away with the idea of a fountain in your "wealth corner" that you forget to allow space for the fridge. If you know you're a bit ditsy in this area, call on a friend (ideally a strong Sensation type) to earth you a bit.

- Thinking types probably won't even be reading this book (it's got pictures!) but if you've been bought this as a present and are reading it out of duty, then maybe just look around your kitchen. Try the exercises and see if you can pinpoint anything that might make it a more exciting space. Allow yourself to create a special environment for once. Play with color, invest in a picture or some ceramics. Start to notice your surroundings.

- If you're a Feeling person, you need to watch out that your home doesn't become overly designed to the point where it becomes unwelcoming. You may also find that you're accumulating hoards of clutter, family furniture, and hand-me-downs. Allow yourself to loosen up, to make sure it's the kind of kitchen where people can drop the occasional crumb and make the odd mark on the table. Choose furniture that can be scrubbed clean and can take a bit of wear and tear.

The Clean, Clear Kitchen

If you've read any of my other books, you'll be sick to death of decluttering. I go on and on about it because it's probably the most simple yet most effective change you can make to a room. It costs nothing to do (and may even make you money) and once it's done I positively guarantee you will feel better and your room will look better.

Kitchens tend to breed "stuff"—almost more than any other room. There are all those jars of spices with a bare sprinkle left; stacks of cook books (and pages torn from magazines with "essential" recipes). There are pots and pans you've had forever—not to mention all the bits and bobs, odds and ends that somehow find their way into drawers and cupboards, on top of the fridge, behind the door.

For the benefit of those who haven't read any of my books, let me very briefly recap why decluttering is such an essential process. On a physical level, clutter attracts dust, which makes many people sneeze or have other allergic reactions. On a psychological level, clutter irritates the mind; it reminds us of

Clear kitchen, clear mind

things that need doing, fixing, finishing, starting even. On an energetic level, the vital energy of the house, its *qi*, becomes confused, sluggish, disordered when it encounters clutter—and our lives follow suit. If you look it up in the dictionary you'll discover that clutter means confusion, a confused heap, turmoil, din. That says it all. When our home environment gets "out of control" we feel disordered in ourselves. Clutter-clearing supremo Karen Kingston puts it this way: "If you have a pile of papers in your room your energy automatically dips because you know it needs attention," and she adds, "every time you walk into your home and there are things that need repairing, letters that need answering, junk that needs clearing, your energy can't flow internally because of what is happening externally."

There is no one way to clear clutter. Personally, I would grab myself a few boxes and rubbish bags and just blitz it. But you may prefer a "softly softly" approach and do a drawer a day, or a week. Whatever—it doesn't matter, as long as you do it. Take a long, hard look at your kitchen. Open up each and every closet and cupboard, each and every drawer. Check behind doors and on top of shelves. Be ruthless.

Let's have a look at the standard types of kitchen clutter and how to deal with them:

COOK BOOKS AND CLIPPINGS: How many cook books does any one soul need? Ten to one you've got so many you could never cook all the dishes they contain in a whole lifetime. Keep the real classics and the ones you use a lot and

send the rest to the charity shop. Go through all those odd bits of paper and clippings and cut out the recipes you want to try. Glue them neatly into an attractive book and you'll have them all at hand. I love the idea of building up your own cook book over the years—sticking in recipes or carefully writing them out with your own notes. It makes a lovely heirloom for your children too. "My mother cooked the best banana loaf/chocolate cookies," etc. is a common refrain—but often we just don't have those elusive recipes. Include photos or (if you're artistic) drawings, as well as short diary entries of who ate the food and when, and you have a thumbnail sketch of meals.

PAPERS: You can't escape bits of paper but you can control them. Always tick the box asking that your details do not go on mailing lists when you send off for products by mail order or enter competitions. Put junk mail straight in the bin—or send it straight back saying you don't want it and to take you off their list. Open your mail standing or sitting by your wastepaper basket and unless it needs a reply or is really useful, put it straight in the bin.

Keep important documents neatly stored in an "essential papers" file and throw any others out. Make sure everything really is essential and go through it once a year to check it's still valid. Kitchens are often the depositories of general household and family "stuff"—letters from school, general junk, etc. Either store it in its rightful place (if it's worth keeping) or get rid of it.

KITCHEN GADGETS: Where do they all come from? There's the gadget that seemed indispensable at the time but now you can't even remember what it does; the gifts you never even wanted; those various fads and fashions—fondue sets, waffle makers, woks, etc. If they're in pristine condition advertise them (someone might be daft enough, and apparently fondues are back in fashion). Otherwise, give them to charity.

OLD EQUIPMENT: Burned-out saucepans, nonstick fry pans that now stick, chipped mugs, the one remaining plate from a set. If they're broken, they're useless. Anything that's chipped, cracked, or broken simply isn't

hygienic—so in the trash with it. Anything else can go to charity.

FOODS/HERBS/SPICES: Go through those cupboards and have a good sort-out. Check those "use-by" dates and throw away anything that's out of date. Herbs and spices tend to lose their pungency as they get older—have a sniff and see (tired herbs will wreck your cooking). Strew old herbs on the fire or barbecue for a lovely scent.

If you tend to have about four packets of opened rice, lentils, or pasta (or whatever)—consolidate by putting it all in large containers with good seals (they will keep the food fresher and save bits of rice escaping all over your cupboards).

FRIDGES/FREEZERS: Keep an eye on use-by dates in your fridge too. And label food as it goes into the freezer so you know when it needs to be used by.

Periodically go through and make sure you're not hoarding useless food.

TOYS/BOOKS/WORK: Kitchens often become storerooms for all kinds of extraneous clutter. Try to make sure you put stuff back in its proper place after you've finished with it. If you do a lot of reading in your kitchen, think about a shelf or bookcase to store books (so they don't litter the table or work surfaces). An attractive box (or a low-level cupboard) is a good storage place for a toddler's toys. It's a nice idea to have a cupboard that your toddler can go into and play with the implements (for some reason, all small children are fascinated with kitchen stuff); pick out pans, sieves, spoons, etc. that won't hurt your child—and that won't get damaged in turn.

If you get really stuck at any point, stop and think how wonderful your kitchen would look without the clutter. Close your eyes and imagine a home that feels free and easy and welcoming. The Chinese sages say that when you throw out clutter you are making room for something new and exciting to come into your life. Hold onto that thought as you bravely clear out the old to make way for the new.

Cleanliness is next to heaven

Few of us actively enjoy cleaning. It's hard work, it's far from glamorous and, to be honest, there are plenty of things we'd rather do with our time. However, of all the rooms in your home, the kitchen is the one that will need most cleaning—so you may as well face up to it and learn to enjoy it.

Cleaning has become almost a dirty word. Yet in the past, it was part and parcel of everyday life. I remember as a child hearing the sound of the vacuum cleaner every day. As I walked to school I would see women (yup, always women) cleaning the front step: first brushing, then buffing it with red tile polish. The door's paint was always freshly washed and the door knocker gleamed. Of course, nowadays we don't have time or we would rather spend what free time we do have in other, more entertaining, ways. So, if we can afford it, we hire someone to clean our space or, if we can't, we fit it in where we can. We race around if guests are coming or wipe a cursory cloth over the worst grime. And so cleaning becomes an activity we begrudge.

Now don't think I'm going to suggest we've got it all wrong and that women should "get back where they belong," i.e., on their hands and knees scrubbing. For a start, cleaning is an occupation for both men and women. But there is a real

need, both physical and spiritual, for clean kitchens—and fortunately there are ways of making the cleaning process far less of a chore.

Serious housework is essential work, not just in terms of cleanliness but for our psyches too. More and more of us earn our livelihood via our heads. If you sit slumped all day in your car or chair, perhaps staring at a computer screen, or battling with machinery, the hard physical graft of cleaning provides a good healthy balance. It plugs us back into the earth, it grounds us.

In many cultures cleaning is considered a form of worship in itself. The Shakers considered work to be good for the soul and a way of glorifying God. "Put your hands to work and your hearts to God," said Ann Lee in a calling cry to the joys of housework. The Shakers performed each task to the highest possible standard, with pride and a sense of joy. It's an inspiring idea.

Housework stops being such a drudge if we imagine we are sweeping out old thoughts, rigid ideas, and moribund emotions along with the dust; that by cleansing the physical environment we are also symbolically purifying our homes of negative and outworn attitudes and feelings. By putting meaning into an everyday task, we bestow it with a sense of the sacred. It becomes ritual rather than chore. Some people say they can use cleaning as a form of meditation.

Think about the following—I find they all make the cleaning process more palatable, and even pleasurable.

- Accept that cleaning is as ephemeral as the wind. But don't use that as an excuse not to bother. After all, flowers don't last forever but that doesn't prevent us bringing them into the house and enjoying their beauty.
- Try to find a regular time for cleaning— even ten minutes a day. Use it as quiet,

home-based time. Focus on one task at a time. Become absorbed in what you are doing. Imagine you are as focused as a Shaker. Be serene when you clean.

- Choose your cleaning tools with care. Pick a good, solid, wooden-handled broom; one that feels comfortable to the grip. Choose sturdy bristle brushes, again with wooden backs. Track down an enamel or tin bucket rather than gaudy plastic. Use natural cotton clothes. Well, those are my preferences. On the other hand, you might be entranced by the vivid colors of modern plastics. It doesn't matter really—choose whatever speaks to your soul and your sense of fun.

- If the idea of quiet contemplative time doesn't appeal, then maybe put on some favorite music. I find I clean far more vigorously to a raunchy rock track—you might prefer Vivaldi. Vacuum to the rhythm, scrub in time. And remember that heavy-duty housework can burn as many calories as a workout—so put some elbow grease into it.

- Modern cleaning materials are synthetic and pretty unpleasant. They do damage to the environment and can cause allergic reactions. They also smell fake. Try to use environmentally-friendly products if you can. You can also make your own (see the "Practical Kitchen" chapter for ideas).

- Using essential oils in cleaning makes the house smell wonderful and perks you up as you clean as well. Wash down paintwork with water to which you've added a few drops of essential oil—or put a couple of drops on your cloth. I use grapefruit on my scrub-top kitchen table. Alternatively, try other fruity oils such as lemon and lime, or the flowery geranium and lavender for a bright summer scent. In winter go for warmer oils such as orange, mandarin, cypress, cedarwood, and rosewood.

The Energetic Kitchen

Even the most avid feng shui fanatic often comes unstuck when confronted with the kitchen. After all, if you need to move your living room furniture around, it's not too tricky. But how the hell do you cope if everything is clamped to the floor and walls in a fully fitted kitchen? Let's take a look at how you can make your kitchen feng shui friendly—or at least cure the worst calamities.

If you're not already familiar with feng shui (you've been on vacation up the Amazon for the past ten years perhaps?), the concept is relatively simple (although the practice is far more complicated). Basically, feng shui developed thousands of years ago in China. People found that they could affect the energy of a building or room by placing things—be it the building itself, a room, or a piece of furniture—in a particular way. This, in turn, caused marked effects on the fortunes of the people using those spaces. Fanciful it may sound, but if you can accept that vital energy (such as the kind experienced in acupuncture and healing) exists, then it becomes logical

that our spaces, as well as our bodies, can be affected by its flow.

Good feng shui can bring myriad benefits; people have found that purely by shifting their living spaces they have become healthier, happier, more wealthy, and even able to find love or conceive a child. So don't dismiss it as mumbo-jumbo until you've tried it for yourself. You'd be in good company; many huge corporations, including banks and hotel chains, use it regularly (if somewhat quietly).

The wealthy, well placed kitchen

Ignore your kitchen feng shui at your peril. In Chinese terms the kitchen is equated with wealth and prosperity, so the state of your cooking space can affect your finances in no uncertain terms. Energy does not care if your kitchen is wildly expensive and in the best possible taste—if it is situated badly your finances will suffer. It also affects your health. Once we are born, food is our form of sustenance, our way of taking in vital energy. How and where the food is prepared is of extreme importance—if the energy of the food is bad, then we are receiving low-grade sustenance and vitality (more on this later in the book).

Unlike other rooms that have specific ideal locations in feng shui, the kitchen can be sited in most areas. In fact, as it is considered such an auspicious room it can augment a part of the house which would otherwise be deemed tricky or difficult. However, there are some exceptions. The kitchen should not be situated in the center of the house for the very practical reason that this prevents smells and steam escaping. It should not face your front door either, as harmful energy coming in from outside could affect it. Equally, it should not open onto your living room or bedroom, as smells will hang over these rooms. If your kitchen is sited in such a way and you can't change it (or don't feel inclined to), then ensure that the doors are kept shut and you have good ventilation. If your kitchen faces the front door, place a small mirror on the kitchen door facing toward the front door to deflect harmful energy.

The ba-gua

Central to feng shui is the ba-gua. This octagonal template (shown opposite) is a map of energy which divides any space—your entire home or simply a room within it—into eight areas. These eight areas, or corners, represent Wealth (finances in general), Fame (how you appear to the outside world), Marriage (and all close relationships), Children (and any other creative process), Helpful People, Career (your path through life),

Knowledge (wisdom, inner knowing, spirituality), and The Family (including your ancestors).

Place the template over a plan of your house—your front door (or the door into your own apartment) will lie on the bottom line (in the areas known as either Knowledge, Career, or Helpful People). Now check where the kitchen falls in your space. If your kitchen is clean and clear (and follows the guidelines in this chapter) it will give an energetic boost to the area in which it falls. If it's cluttered, dirty, and ill-working, that area will cause problems in your life.

WEALTH: A highly auspicious place for a kitchen—prosperity and general abundance should follow. Make sure you share your blessings with other people, particularly those less favored than yourself. Be thoughtful and invite isolated relatives and lonely neighbors for supper once in a while.

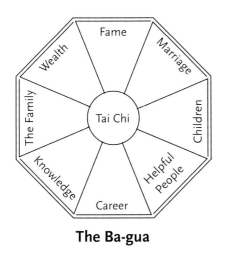

The Ba-gua

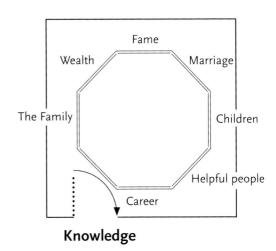

Knowledge

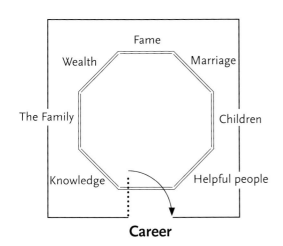

Career

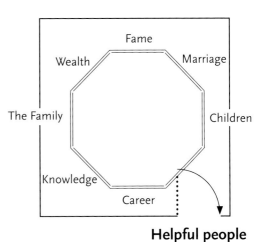

Helpful people

FAMILY: A great placing if you have a family (or if you want one). It also welcomes in strangers and the wider community so you should have a sociable life. You may need to ensure you have time for yourself though—this kitchen can be wildly sociable.

KNOWLEDGE: You'll be able to focus on self-improvement, wisdom, and knowledge. Be wary, however, of becoming too inward in focus. Make an effort to have people around, to sit and talk rather than keep your nose in a book.

FAME: You should enjoy a good reputation and find acknowledgment in your life. Boost the energy of this area and you may even enjoy a certain amount of fame. It's another sociable place for a kitchen, but watch out the cook doesn't become overbearing and egotistical.

MARRIAGE: A good kitchen in this area augurs well for all relationships, whether you are married or not. This is a wonderful area for entertaining—whether it's romantic candlelit dinners or family get-togethers. Be careful, however, that other people don't feel left out.

CHILDREN: Also known as Creativity, this area is a good place for a family kitchen and should also prove a place where you can let your imagination run wild, be it in creative cookery or other artistic endeavors. If you do have children, watch out that it doesn't become overrun with their stuff.

HELPFUL PEOPLE: Again, the implications are obvious. A good kitchen in this spot should ensure you find help from unexpected places. People greet you with a smile and show a willingness to help. However, allow this kitchen to get cluttered and you'll find frustrations around every corner.

CAREER: This area is not just about work but how you journey through life, so it's incredibly important. A good kitchen here can support your ambitions and help you on your journey. In contrast, if you allow clutter to gather here life will seem like an uphill struggle.

The clutter-free kitchen

You'll notice the word "clutter" is coming up again. Clutter is anathema to feng shui. Energy becomes stuck where there is lots of "stuff" hanging around, so do follow the guidelines in the previous chapter. As far as possible keep your work surfaces (and all other surfaces) clear. A touch of minimalism in the kitchen is no bad thing. If you leave things out they will quickly become greasy and dirty and will need constant cleaning. It's far better to have everything stowed in cupboards within easy reach so you can take them out as needed. By all means have "things" in your kitchen but keep them away from the food preparation side of things.

In particular, make sure knives are kept safely stowed in a drawer. It's common to see knives displayed in kitchens, in racks or along the back of a butcher's block. In feng shui terms, knives (and all sharp objects) throw out "cutting *qi*" which can cause arguments, unease, and general bad luck. If you have children, remember to keep all sharp utensils in inaccessible places with childproof locks on them.

Placement in the kitchen

The most important part of your kitchen is your oven. Remember, this is the symbolic hearth, the heart of your home. Unfortunately, feng shui rules for siting ovens are often hard to follow in the modern home. In an ideal world, your oven would be placed so you could see people coming into the kitchen as you worked. It should not be placed opposite the sink or fridge, as this direct opposition of fire and water is considered inauspicious. An island arrangement is a good solution but there should not be too much space for people to walk behind the chef.

If you find your oven or any area where you spend a lot of time is in a tricky spot (i.e., your back is to the door), then place a mirror so you can see the door behind you. A mirrored sheet or reflective metal behind the oven is considered highly beneficial in its own right as it symbolically doubles the number of burners you have. The more burners you have, the more auspicious for your finances. But make sure you use all of them.

Feng shui follows the standard practice for siting a sink—ideally in front of the window so you can look out and the steam can safely evaporate. Curiously, stainless steel is considered auspicious and symbolic of prosperity, so don't race to replace yours. Make sure your sink is always spotlessly clean and unblocked. In feng shui terms, plumbing relates to your intestines and (once again) finances, so blocked plumbing of any kind may translate into sluggish bowels and a sluggish bank balance.

There are a few other points that are easily followed, so do try these in your kitchen space:

- Keep a lid on your kitchen bin at all times. Don't allow it to become full and overflowing, as this symbolically rubbishes your life.
- Units and tables should have soft, rounded edges to prevent argumentative cutting *qi*.
- Beams are a feng shui nightmare. Soften them with garlands of hops or drying herbs—and don't spend a lot of time directly underneath them or your health will suffer.

- Keep materials natural. Don't have too much metal or it will overpower the kitchen's governing Earth energy.
- Hang a crystal in your kitchen window to attract positive energy.
- Kitchens should be well lit with a variety of light options.
- Ventilation should be good too. Open windows are always preferable but if you need an extractor fan, do shop around for one that is not too noisy and obtrusive.

The Practical Kitchen

So far, our kitchen deliberations have been pretty esoteric. Now it's time to get a bit more practical. Having figured out your soul needs, it's time to put them into practice. But before you start racing out and ordering units, refrigerator and all, let's make sure your choices are going to be healthy for you and your family.

One point many people overlook is the actual height of their work surfaces. If you are particularly tall or short—or anything other than what kitchen manufacturers consider "average"—you will probably be working in a very uncomfortable position. Consider having your work surfaces raised or lowered to suit you (of course, if you share your kitchen with people of varying heights this can be tricky and you'll need to compromise). If you have the space, you could designate different areas for each of you. Work surfaces should be generous and wide so you have enough space to chop and prepare. And have a double sink if possible—so you can keep dish washing and preparing food quite separate.

Think carefully about what units you actually need and will use. We tend to follow fashion blindly and kitchen design companies usually tend to fill every available inch of kitchen space with units (it makes sense for them—the more units they sell, the more money they make). But a less packed kitchen can look wonderful and feel spacious. You might think about free-standing units, these are often beautiful pieces of furniture in their own right. Alternatively, a simple row of floor cabinets might fulfill your needs, leaving your walls blank for the stunning impact of some fabulous color—or an obvious canvas for works of art (who says the kitchen can't have paintings?).

The waste-less kitchen

When planning a kitchen, you need to think about far more than just units and major appliances. For instance, where are you going to put your waste? If we all recycled our waste (and there is a heck of a lot of kitchen waste) we could live far more lightly on this planet. Let's think about simple ways of helping in this process:

- Try, if possible, to buy food as lightly packaged as possible.
- Fresh food straight from the producer (I know it's not always easy but do try) tends to come in a biodegradable paper bag, rather than several layers of plastic and polyurethane.
- Sort your rubbish into separate bins: paper, plastics, glass, metal, organic waste—and recycle whatever you can.
- Compost all your kitchen organic waste (with the exception of potatoes). If possible, have a composting bin near your kitchen door.
- Pick glass rather than plastic wherever possible and recycle.

The natural kitchen

We spend our time trying to ensure our kitchens are hygienic and healthy yet many of us are actually working in highly toxic spaces. Before you buy that new kitchen, let's look at the hazards it might be hiding—and the kind of choices that support a healthful, natural kitchen.

KITCHEN UNITS: Plywood, chipboard, MDF, and other composites used in units can contain formaldehyde (which can in turn contaminate your food). MDF is beloved of kitchen designers because it is so cheap and versatile but, when you consider the noxious gases that leach from it, you may prefer to choose a more expensive, and perhaps less flexible option for the kitchen (or indeed any room in the house). Natural, untreated wood is the safest answer but if you don't have any choice in the matter seal surfaces with nontoxic paint or varnish and thoroughly ventilate the kitchen.

WORK SURFACES: Laminates can give off noxious fumes too. Try to find alternative work surfaces such as solid wood, slate, ceramic tiles, marble, or stainless steel. All of these look wonderful but can be pricey. Try your local reclamation center or cabinet maker for solid wood surfaces. Slate can look fabulous too, while stainless steel is the obvious choice for industrial-chic kitchens.

FLOORING: Laminate flooring and vinyl tiles also give off vapors. Think instead about ceramic tiles, stone, sealed cork, linoleum, or natural wood (either reclaimed boards or sealed timber strip). Stone and ceramic floors can be very unforgiving if you have small children— or if you drop a piece of precious china or glassware. Reclaimed wood floors are great—they can be painted or stained to fit in with pretty well any décor, whether clear modern kitchen or cozy farmhouse variety. Linoleum (marmoleum) is another brilliant choice for kitchens. It's incredibly hygienic, totally natural, plus it comes in a huge array of patterns, colors, and styles.

WALLS, DOORS, WINDOWS: Paints, varnishes, and adhesives can be the hidden cause behind many allergies and illnesses. Try to pick natural nontoxic ranges—many now have a wide range of

colors. Don't worry about special kitchen paint—normal finishes work just as well and most people tend to have tiles or splashboards where the worst spillages are likely to happen. Okay, you may have to decorate a little more often, but ten to one by the time you need to repaint the walls you'll be itching for a change of color or style anyhow.

STOVES: Gas, coal, and wood-burning stoves produce a range of combustion by-products such as carbon monoxide and nitrogen dioxide. Open the windows while cooking or, if this isn't possible, install an extractor fan and hood over the stove. Make sure all cooking appliances are regularly checked and serviced. The AGA brand and similar range oven-stoves are undoubtedly expensive but can be a great investment. Despite the fact that they are on all the time (which you might think leads to huge fuel bills) they are so energy efficient you will actually save

money. They also make a wonderful surrogate "hearth." I think the AGA phenomenon in England, where I live, is really interesting. People talk about their AGAs as almost a member of the family, investing them with personalities and even talking to them. Why not? Probably they are unconsciously recognizing the importance of the primal hearth and worshipping it in their own way.

Now to the thorny question of microwaves. However much people may try to persuade me they're safe, I still feel they are a potential radiation hazard and I just can't believe that "zapping" food in this way is anything other than a travesty. I have never had one in my kitchen and never would. If I don't have time for a properly cooked meal, I'd rather opt for a sandwich than fling a frozen dinner in a microwave. And if you never have time for "proper" cooking then I'd suggest you need to look at your lifestyle and your stress levels.

FRIDGES/FREEZERS AND OTHER APPLIANCES: What can I say? We can't bear the idea of living without them but they are real energy guzzlers. If you're buying anything new for the kitchen, do check out its energy rating and please choose the one that is the most gentle on the environment. This is one area where I would always advise you to buy new, rather than recycle the old. Old appliances generally are far more energy-greedy. Make sure they are disposed of carefully as well.

POTS AND PANS: Some experts believe that aluminum pots and pans increase the risk of Alzheimer's disease. Copper pans are beloved of many chefs but, while they may look gorgeous, they can easily build up verdigris, which is pretty toxic. If you do use copper, make sure it is meticulously clean. Otherwise, if you want to be entirely safe, choose stainless steel, cast iron, enamel, cook-proof glass, or earthenware for your cooking needs.

Cleaning the kitchen

Virtually everything you buy to clean your kitchen, whether it's dishwasher detergent or liquid soap, drain cleaner or bleach, fabric softeners or scouring cleanser, contains toxic chemicals. Yes, they're easy and highly effective but there are alternatives which are kinder both to the environment and your own health.

- Clean fridges and freezers with hot lemon juice and water (equal proportions of each).

- Make windows sparkle by adding clear vinegar to water (one third vinegar to two thirds water). Polish with newspaper when nearly dry (I know it sounds mad but it works, honestly).
- Clean chopping boards with a little salt and water, then rinse. Lemon juice and salt, or vinegar, are good deodorizers.
- Instead of disinfectant, try adding tea tree oil (a natural disinfectant) to white vinegar—about ten drops to a bottle of vinegar.

- Cleaning drains is extremely hazardous as store-bought products are highly toxic and dangerous. Instead, pour half a cup of baking soda into the drain and then add a cup of white vinegar. Cover until the fizzing stops. Rinse with boiling water.
- For general-purpose kitchen cleaning, simply use baking soda with a little essential oil added to make it smell fresh (remember, mostly we buy cleaning products because they smell nice—so psychologically we think they are doing their job). You can choose whichever oils you like but the citrus ones (grapefruit, lemon, orange, lime) are refreshing; pine is uplifting and smells satisfyingly "medicinal."

I don't have space to go into every alternative. If you're interested I recommend you get hold of *Clean House, Clean Planet* (see "Further Reading"), which will really open your eyes to the horrible products we use in our kitchens—and how to avoid them. One note of extreme caution: If you do use kitchen chemicals and have children, please ensure they are stored safely. Ideally, put them in a locked cupboard as high up as possible (remember, children can climb and can be incredibly curious). Most kitchen cleaning products are extremely dangerous and can cause burns, blindness, internal damage, or even death if spilled on skin, put in eyes, or swallowed.

Kitchen of the Senses

Your kitchen should indulge all your senses. In fact, of all the rooms in the house, it has the most potential to be a sensory palace. Let's think about the perfect kitchen. The first thing you notice as you walk in is the scent. A symphony of smells assails your nose—hopefully in the nicest possible way. Your taste buds and stomach perk up in anticipation and you look around for the source. As you look, your eyes notice how inviting the kitchen looks. It simply begs you to walk in, look at things: that interesting painting on the wall, the amusing fridge magnet, the farm animal cut-outs the children made at school which are decorating the cupboard door. Your hand reaches out and feels the rippled slate on the surfaces. You pick up a peach from the beautiful glass bowl and gently stroke its downy skin across your cheek before sinking your teeth in. Maybe you sit down at the table and watch the cook. He or she pours you a glass of wine, or home-made lemonade, or freshly brewed coffee—and you listen to the sounds of· the kitchen. Something is sizzling in the frying pan and, if you listen carefully, you can hear the quiet bubbles of a simmering pot of soup. Your chef may hand you a bowl of peas to shell and you're plunged back into a childhood memory of the bumpy pods and the shiny wonder of the peas as they pop out. There's no hurry, you're just enjoying being in the moment.

But I don't have time for all that, I can almost hear you saying. Well, not all the time, of course. But even when you're in a tearing hurry, your kitchen should have the power to entice your senses and, in so doing, anchor you in the moment (which is a healing process in itself).

Let's take a look at how you can indulge all your senses in the kitchen.

Sight

Yes, a kitchen should look good. As I've said, how you decorate is up to you but don't let yourself be caught up by convention or fashion. Think about color first of all; kitchens traditionally tended to be white or yellow, sometimes blue—but whatever the color it was usually in soft tones. These days there are no real rules. I adore my vibrant green kitchen (with its red AGA, white units, and electric-blue chairs and door handles). It sounds odd but it works (nobody was more surprised than I was). I've seen a wonderful candy-pink kitchen and an equally stunning kitchen painted in Etruscan orange tones with vibrant blue units. Then again, some dear friends of mine have a serene kitchen painted off-white, with warm wood units, and a stone floor of myriad hues. Look for color inspiration everywhere you go. As I've said, mine came from young beech leaves, but you might be drawn by a sunset, or a piece of glass or china, or some ethnic fabric, or your child's building bricks.

If you're planning your kitchen from scratch, do think about ordering custom-made cabinets, or buying free-standing furniture. Until I moved to the country, I never even considered buying from anything other than a store and anything other than ready-made. But, living far away from the stores, I soon found that local craftspeople can usually undercut their prices anyway (you're cutting out the middle-man and all those overheads) and, even better, you are getting a well-crafted, custom item that is exactly what you want. Most cabinet makers have a huge reverence for their work and tend to use wood, although many will work with whatever materials you require. (Remember if you do use fiberboard that you will need to seal it with natural paint and varnishes and keep the room aired for many months to minimize the toxic fumes.) Many cabinet-makers will happily work with reclaimed wood—or possibly with local timber. I heard a lovely tale of a family who had an ancient oak in their garden. The tree had died and was becoming dangerous but the family were bereft at the thought of using their old friend for firewood. Then they had the idea of using its wood for a kitchen—and a local craftsman made wonderful cabinets, closets, chairs, and a large table from the venerable oak. Ensure that any wood that is used, or that you buy, comes from sustainable sources and isn't contributing to the destruction of the rainforests. You might feel drawn to planting some trees to replace that used in your kitchen.

If you're stuck with your existing kitchen, don't despair. You have two choices. Replacing the doors of your units is a great solution, particularly if the structure of the kitchen is sound but you just can't stand the old-fashioned look. Again, someone local may well be able to do the job far cheaper and more aesthetically than the mass-market firms that make replacement doors. If your budget won't even rise to that, then get out your paintbrush. My own kitchen units were a brown wood-effect which made the kitchen incredibly dark. We simply painted them in a clear, crisp white and added bright blue handles. We also painted the tiles. It cost next to nothing and made a vast improvement.

How do you clad your walls? Personally, I think paint really is the best option in the humid atmosphere of a kitchen. Having said that, there are some fabulous wallpapers around which might prove tempting, particularly if you're after a retro feel for your space. However, if your kitchen tends to get very steamy, you might end up fighting a losing battle. I don't advocate either paints or papers specifically designed for kitchens as they don't allow walls to breathe and so set up further problems.

The kitchen is one place where even quite conservative types feel they can be slightly wilder and wackier. If you can't pluck up the nerve to go wild with units or walls, dip a toe into a more colorful world with your accessories. Here are just a few suggestions:

- Why have all your chairs the same color when you could have one of each?
- Why have a white refrigerator when you could have a pretty pink one, or a brilliant orange one?
- If you have an all-white kitchen, a display of mugs, glasses, or bowls, either all one stunning color or a rainbow selection of many, can look fabulous.
- Think bold and bright for your art. Maybe go beyond the standard, slightly sweet, kitchenalia and plump for some huge modern prints, nicely framed. Alternatively, frame your own, or your children's art.
- The kitchen is a great place to display photographs, but don't let them get cluttered. Maybe devote a whole wall to family pics, beautifully framed, or make a collage. You could also simply display

your favorite pics laminated (black and white works really well)— this prevents them from getting sticky.

- Go wild with fabric. Wildly printed fabric makes great tablecloths. Choose sweet fifties-style prints or sixties graphics; bold, big patterns or animal prints. Some ethnic fabrics come in stunning colors which will brighten up any kitchen.

- Candles have a natural place in the kitchen and can make an instant design statement—whether you pick dazzling electric blue, sophisticated dark brown, or cool, clean cream.

Sound

The kitchen has its own set of natural sounds. Notice the sound of chopping, of slicing, of frying, simmering, boiling. The sizzle of the roasting pan as it comes out of the oven. Whether you introduce other sounds into your kitchen is a matter of choice. My husband always has the radio on or listens to his favorite classical music. Some might enjoy listening to a play or spoken-word cassette. I like music if I'm doing something prosaic like cleaning, but prefer my own meditative thoughts if I'm cooking. If you have a radio in the kitchen, maybe go for a battery-operated one which can be moved around, and sit near the sink with impunity. I'm not a huge fan of televisions in the kitchen (Hermes again) though my young son heartily disagrees and adores it when we visit people who watch the box over breakfast. It's up to you, but try not to have it on all the time (and particularly not at mealtimes).

Scent

Why do people use air fresheners and odor busters in the kitchen? Good food, carefully prepared, has its own wondrous scent. If you fry a lot you will undoubtedly create less pleasant odors (one additional reason to cut down on frying—quite apart from the health perils). But luxuriate in the scent of good food and indulge those practices which make the best smells of all: home baking. Is there anything to beat the scent of freshly baked bread? I'm hard-pressed to think of anything, although freshly brewed coffee is pretty excellent and I shamefully confess to be addicted to the scent of sizzling bacon. Home baking is real domestic goddess stuff and we'll look a little more at it in the chapters which follow. Here are some more odoriferous ideas:

- If you can, find a spot just outside the kitchen door, or on the windowsill for a few tubs of herbs. Chives, marjoram, parsley, thyme, dill, and cilantro will all sit nicely in a windowbox. You might prefer to keep mint in a separate pot as it is incredibly invasive. Rosemary, bay, and sage will be happy in pots too, though they grow big so will need transplanting after a few years. The scent is wonderful, they deter bugs and, if you need herbs for your recipes, all you need do is lean out the window and snip.
- Harvest herbs for winter use and hang them in loosely tied bundles in a warm place. Again, their scent will permeate your kitchen.
- If you do find your kitchen gets a bit smelly (in the bad sense), shun

Touch

chemicals in favor of natural deodorants. Burn some essential oils— lemon, grapefruit, mandarin, and geranium are lovely in kitchens.

- Always make space for some flowers in your kitchen—choose them for color and scent.
- I always put a few drops of lavender and rosemary oil in my drawers to deter moths and other creepy-crawlies. They smell divine too.

There's nothing better than a touchy-feely kitchen. How does the floor feel under your feet? Do your fingers want to stroke the tabletop? Think about the undulating surface of an ancient wood chopping block. Try to introduce various textures and surfaces to your kitchen. If you have good walls, why not leave the brick bare—or simply add a coat of paint. Some friends of mine have a wonderful kitchen with bare brick walls. A place I

stayed on vacation had raw stone walls—very elemental.

If you can't introduce much in the way of texture and touch to your basic kitchen infrastructure, again think of the details:

- Beautiful bowls made of ceramic, stone, glass, papier mâché (make your own with the children and embed dried flowers, herbs, or leaves into the structure).
- Willow baskets make great kitchen storage—we use them for stowing papers for recycling.
- Have fun with fabrics again—fake zebra-skin chair covers or fake fur cushions?
- Curtains aren't great in kitchens as they trap grease, but blinds work well. Wooden venetian blinds or shutters feel and look good; some companies make inventive ones with holes in attractive patterns. They let the light fall in interesting ways and feel intriguing too.
- A slab of marble is wonderful for pastry-making and feels sublimely cool on hot days.
- Mosaic as a splashboard is different and feels unusual too.

Taste

Oh, come on! You can do this bit for yourself. I'm not going to say much here except that it's always a great idea to have a huge bowl of seasonal fruit on the table at all times and a jar full of home-made cookies or brownies in case hunger pangs strike. Other than that, it's over to you.

Eating meditation

If you really want to get in touch with your senses, I'd suggest trying this simple exercise. It's also a great introduction to the chapters that follow. Jon Kabat-Zinn, PhD, of the Stress Reduction Clinic at the University of Massachusetts Medical Center, suggests practicing mindfulness meditation while you eat. Not only does it plug you right into the moment, but it also helps to foster the correct relationship between your mind and your food.

1 Look at a piece of food—say, a raisin. Imagine you are an alien scientist who has arrived on earth and never seen one before. What do you see?

2 Now smell it. What is its scent? Really think about it.

3 Now notice the physiological reaction in your mouth. You might be salivating already as a reaction to the anticipation of the food.

4 Now explore how the raisin feels.

5 Think about how your hand will bring the raisin to your lips. How does your hand know how to deliver the raisin to your mouth? Be aware of this motion as you bring the raisin up to and into your mouth.

6 Bite into the raisin consciously, slowly. Start to chew. How do you chew? How does it taste? There are hundreds of words to describe taste—really think about it.

7 As you chew, the taste changes. So does the consistency. What is the texture of the raisin?

8 Don't swallow yet, even though you might well want to. Become aware of any aversion. Now swallow, following the path of the raisin to the back of your mouth. Then, in your mind's eye, follow it down into the stomach. Become aware that you are now one raisin heavier.

The Alchemical Kitchen

Alchemy is the art of transformation, of changing a set of ingredients into something entirely different and new. The medieval alchemists were supposedly searching to find a means of transmuting base metal into gold. However, a more subtle explanation is that they were actually looking to transform their very selves and souls; to shift themselves from the base material of earthly life to a purer, more spiritual state. I think that, for our purposes, it's worth keeping both ideas in mind. Cooking is an alchemical process—of that there is no doubt. You take a bunch of diverse ingredients, chop them, cook them, blend them, season, and spice them—and they emerge from the oven transformed into something quite different. Good cooking is more, far more, than mere culinary sleight of hand; it's not that kind of magic. Good food is soul food—it nourishes us not just physically but on a deep emotional, psychic and, yes, magical level.

It is quite fascinating that scientists are now turning their attention to the links between food and consciousness. It seems that how we prepare our food is

just as important as what we choose to eat. Dr Larry Dossey, a scientist investigating the link between science and spirituality, says, "That our consciousness affects matter (including food) is not in doubt. How it happens is a huge mystery." Physicist Fred Alan Wolf, PhD, says it is insufficient to ask, "What nutrients are in the food?" Rather, we should be asking, "What were you thinking about when you were eating?"

A new scientific field is in the making—one that may give us a prescription for creating an, as yet, unidentified "nutrient" that manifests through the wisdom and awareness we bring to our food. Numerous experiments have shown that healing can increase the energy and growing capacity of seeds and can even keep milk fresh for longer. Dr Leonard Laskow, a leading researcher in the field and author of

Healing with Love, discovered that by combining intention, visualization, and healing energy, food could be transformed—it could literally contain more vitality, more healing power. Projecting loving energy to an orange actually changed the taste and texture of the fruit—it peeled more easily and was juicier and sweeter. "Spiritually imbued" cheap wine took on the taste of a classic vintage.

Try the following to test the potential of spiritually imbued food.

- Processed vs hand-prepared vegetables. Make a salad: chop half of the vegetables by hand using a knife and cutting board, and chop the other half in a food processor. Can you detect the difference?
- Cooking consciously vs unconsciously. Before enjoying a favorite dish, choose the ingredients, and prepare, cook,

Creating food with loving energy

and eat the food with a loving consciousness. As a contrast, next time you prepare the same dish, choose to do so during an especially busy time—so everything is done in a hurry, without any care or thought. Can you detect any difference?

Here's how to infuse food and liquids with loving, spiritual energy.

1 Become aware of your breathing. Give yourself permission to relax in both mind and body.

2 Focus your attention on the area around your heart, imagining you are breathing

Baking bread

in and out through that chakra (or energy center). Bring to mind deep, loving, and caring feelings (you may remember a time with a special person, or how you feel when you listen to a particularly moving piece of music).

3 Now envisage a shimmering sphere of light several inches above your head (at the crown chakra). Imagine the energy from this glistening light entering through the crown of your head, cascading down to your heart and hands, then overflowing out through your heart and hands.

4 Now project this energy into the food or drink. Visualize the light coming out through your heart and hands and infusing the food, like a searchlight. Surround both sides of the dish or glass with your hands and imagine energy coming from both hands into the food or drink.

To my mind, one of the most magical and alchemical of cooking practices is that of baking bread. It may be time-consuming and I'm not advocating you do it every day—although you can buy bread-makers now that will provide you with bread with minimal effort. They are a nifty invention and one of the exceptions (along with juicers) to my general anti-gadget stance, but every once in a while do make your bread the old-fashioned way, as it is way more therapeutic.

Next time you find yourself ready to explode, don't take it out on the family— beat up some bread! Baking bread is about as primal a therapy as you can get. Honestly, there's nothing that matches pounding your fists into the bouncy dough; slapping it down onto the table with a resounding thwack; chucking it around the kitchen (with accompanying grunts, groans, and gripes). It beats kick-boxing any day—and is much safer.

There's something miraculous about bread. It's about as earthy as food gets yet is also highly spiritual fare. "As a source of sustenance for thousands of years, bread signifies an essential, basic food, the 'staff of life' that provided spiritual nourishment and sustenance for the human soul," says nutritionist Deborah Kesten (see "Further Reading" for her book). Most of the great religions consider bread sacred fare. Christianity is nourished by bread—not just the miracle of the loaves and fishes but the Last Supper, which was the original Holy Communion. At a typical Polish wedding feast, the priest will bless the *kolacze*, a flat, plaited loaf of bread that symbolizes all bread—the staff of life. Muslims hold bread to be God's bounty—deserving of respect and veneration at all times. Likewise, in the Jewish tradition, unleavened (yeast-free) bread is seen as a gift from God.

Yet I like bread-making for more basic reasons: primarily because it has the capacity to bring you back down to earth in minutes. If I've been stuck in my head, working for hours on my computer and feeling somewhat "spacey," bread-making is the antidote. It's physical in the extreme but also wondrously magical. Bread is pure alchemy; it rises before your very eyes, and I like to imagine all my stupid angers and petty irritations rising with it until they become so light they simply float away.

A few years ago, I used to spend a lot of time at a wonderful place called the Pelican Centre (now sadly closed). Run by Jungian psychotherapist Jane Mayers, it hosted silent retreats, art therapy courses, and other forms of therapy. One thing Jane always insisted on was fresh bread every day. In fact, if you were feeling really low, she would sneak you

out of whatever you were doing and pull you into the kitchen to bake. She reckoned it was soul therapy in itself—and I heartily agree. Here's her recipe for Pelican rolls: a nutty, earthy, totally delicious bread (and the recipe is virtually fool-proof).

1 Put a small handful of yeast in a bowl and add a spoonful of sugar and a little warm water (from a measured 2 $\frac{1}{2}$ cups/1 UK pint). Mix and hear it bubble.

2 Heat your oven to 180°C/350°F/Gas mark 6.

3 Put a packet (2.2 pounds/1kg) of granary malted flour in another bowl. Scatter half a tablespoon of sea salt over the flour and add around two

tablespoons of olive oil. Now add the rest of the warm water.

4 Pour the yeast mixture over the flour mixture. Squeeze and knead the bread together (this recipe doesn't need masses of kneading if you are short on time).

5 Leave to rise in a warm spot for ten minutes. Break into rolls (if you're feeling clever you can plait them or make mini cottage loaves).

6 Bake for 20–24 minutes. To test, take one out and tap the bottom—if it sounds hollow, they're done.

7 Now all you have to do is eat them (preferably still warm) with a comforting bowl of soup, a slab of sharp tangy cheese or just—forget the diet for once—a dollop of butter.

Composting

Another alchemical process comes at the end of the cooking cycle. If you possibly can, try to compost your kitchen waste. Any organic matter (vegetable scrapings and peelings, leftovers, etc.) can be put into a composter and left to break down into lovely garden fertilizer. Technically, you can compost anything (except potatoes, which will sprout) but many people prefer not to compost meat as it takes longer to break down and can attract scavengers. You will need to turn your compost regularly (or buy a wormery in which the worms will do all the work for you). If you have a garden, it's a great way of saving money. If you don't, donate your fertilizer to someone who does.

The Kitchen Temple

By now you have hopefully realized that your kitchen is way more than just a place in which to heat up a frozen dinner or to show off your fancy gadgetry. A kitchen is a place in which you prepare food—our earthly and spiritual sustenance. Food has been linked with the sacred since time began. It is only in recent years that we have lost our connection with the food that sustains us. Nowadays many of us barely register what we eat; we eat on the run, gulping down "fast food"; we pop "convenience food" in the microwave and unconsciously swallow it while watching television. Few of us sit down as a family to enjoy good food.

All the great religions teach that food is a blessing from the Divine and should be treated with immense respect and gratitude. No religious Jewish, Christian, Hindu, Muslim, or Buddhist family would dream of just tucking into a meal without saying a blessing and giving thanks. In China, food is considered to be a physical link between humans and the gods; beautifully prepared meals are given as a sacred offering on family

altars. In the ayurvedic tradition of India, food is a spiritual science with precise prescriptions of how to prepare and eat food for physical, emotional, and spiritual well-being. In African-American culture there is the tradition of "soul food." Soul food is food cooked with love, intent, intuition, and a sense of history. It is a living prayer and celebration, and has much to teach.

Although the individual rituals and customs may vary, all these traditions have several things in common. First, they recognize that food is far more than mere fuel for the body; it also sustains the soul. Second, they believe in the mindful planning, preparation, and consumption of food. Third, they insist on the necessity to give thanks for the food we eat. Most of them also sanctify the ritual of eating together in groups—whether of friends or family.

Until the twentieth century, the hearth had always been the center of the home. It was the kitchen center around which the family kept warm, fed itself, and discussed the day's work. At day's end, family members gathered in the kitchen, preparing and eating their meals, praying, laughing, and planning. Start to rekindle the idea of the kitchen hearth in your home. Inspire family and friends to pull together for their physical, mental, and spiritual nourishment, particularly at mealtimes.

- If you never eat together, start up a ritual of at least one family mealtime per week. Gradually, as it becomes enjoyable, move it to once a day (and beyond if possible).
- Give a prayer or ask for blessing of some kind before you start to cook. Prepare yourself by mindfully washing your hands and putting on your vestments (apron!). Assemble your tools and ingredients carefully. You might want to light a candle or an aromatherapy burner.
- Before you eat, say grace of some form. Maybe think about where your food has come from and thank the crops, the animals, the fish—and Mother Earth herself. Take it in turns to say grace.
- Meals should be sociable occasions—lively conversation is great. Ensure everyone is included.
- Mealtimes may be the only chance for couples or families to discuss issues—don't let them degenerate into slagging matches though. If things get heated, use a talking stick. Only the person holding the stick can speak and when he or she is finished, the stick is passed to someone else who can pick it up and speak.

Creating the kitchen temple

Any space that is dedicated to a sacred purpose and used mindfully can be a temple. It doesn't need special hangings or furniture—and I'm not going to suggest you waft incense around it (I find it gives a rather odd taste to the food). Your intention is all that really counts.

You may, however, like to space cleanse your kitchen (see *Spirit of the Living Room*) and then dedicate it to the purpose of joyful sustenance, communication, and community (a true marriage of Hestia and Hermes).

A kitchen altar is a great idea. Many kitchens already have them, almost unconsciously, in the form of displays of photos and artwork on a bulletin-board or a selection of pleasing objects on the windowsill or on top of the fridge. I like to create seasonal altars on my kitchen windowsill. They are very simple: a few candles, an aromatherapy burner (essential oils give a wonderful mood and also help to remove cooking smells from the kitchen), bits and pieces my son James and I have picked up outside (a feather, a vase of wild flowers, nuts and berries, an abandoned nest, a beautiful stone, or piece of wood). Come the festival of Halloween on October 31st, I put up pictures of those who have passed away so we can remember them and send our love.

What you put in or on your altar is entirely up to you, but you might like to think about the following:

• A corn dolly or a few ears of corn to honor Demeter.
• A figurine of the Earth Goddess or other deities.

- Yellow candles to symbolize warmth and friendship (and also to honor Hestia as a symbolic hearth). If it's safe to do so, you might consider keeping a candle burning through the day (in a bowl of water or sand for safety).
- A pot of salt (useful but also symbolic of Earth).
- Bundles of dried herbs (again, handy for cooking but also have their own symbolism and bring their particular energies to your kitchen). Sage represents wisdom, thyme is purifying, dill brings prosperity, and fennel helps guard against negativity.

- It's always lovely to have fresh, bright flowers on the altar—and they brighten up the kitchen too. The kitchen is a seasonal place so try to pick local flowers in season (rather than exotics flown in from far away).
- Photos of your family.
- Arts and crafts made by you or your children. An altar is a lovely place to celebrate your children's creativity and it makes them feel valued.

Although we're not going to turn our kitchens into churches, it can feel right to add a few spiritual touches to remind ourselves of the spirituality of food and cooking.

- Start thinking of your kitchen as sacred space. Put something that reminds you of that on your kitchen door: maybe a sacred symbol, a mandala, an angel, a favorite saying or prayer.
- Include images that inspire you in the kitchen. It doesn't need to be the rather hackneyed naïve animals or botanicals—how about a beautiful mandala, the Tree of Life, an icon, representations of the chakras, or the Buddha or other deities?
- Some charts can be very useful: a poster giving the uses of herbs (both culinary and magical) could be handy, but frame it nicely so it doesn't get dog-eared or splattered.
- Candles give a temple feel—choose beautiful candlesticks and place carefully so they won't get in the way while you're cooking or be knocked over.
- Lay your table with care and thought. Think of each person as you lay their place and send out love and whatever else they may need—courage, patience, hope, etc. Little gestures, like tying a strand of lavender around a napkin as an impromptu napkin ring, make people smile (and it smells nice). Always have a candle on the table (not so tall it obstructs your view of people) and a little vase of wild flowers is nice, or perhaps petals strewn over the tablecloth. How about putting little messages or lines from poems on each person's place setting?
- Arrange your food with care—good presentation makes food appetizing and harks back to the idea of food as a gift to the gods. Use edible flowers and herbs to garnish dishes or be fanciful in the way you present food—children in particular adore a "picture" on their plate.

Kitchen farewell

Sadly, we've come to the end of this little book. There is so much more I could say about a kitchen with spirit and soul, but I guess you will discover plenty for yourself once you start to cook and eat with care and consideration.

I hope I have given you "food for thought" and some inspiration for your own kitchen temple. All that remains is for me to sit down with a cup of freshly brewed coffee and maybe a freshly baked cookie and to wish a blessing upon you in your own kitchen. May you always have good food to eat and good friends and family to share it. Blessed be.

Resources

Food in General

If you're interested in the deeper philosophy of food, I'd recommend the following books.

• *Feeding the Body, Nourishing the Soul* by Deborah Kesten (Conari Press). An absolutely fabulous book which looks at both ancient tradition and cutting-edge science and puts it all together in a totally beguiling way.

• *Tasting Food, Tasting Freedom* by Sidney W. Mintz (Beacon Press). Fascinating essays by an anthropologist looking at how we eat and what we eat—and what those choices mean.

• *The Sacred Kitchen* by Robin Robertson and Jon Robertson (New World Library). A book that's very much on my own wavelength with talk of alchemy, feng shui, and ritual—plus it has recipes.

• *The Ancient Cookfire* by Carrie L'Esperance (Bear & Co.) is packed with ideas and recipes for rejuvenating body and spirit through seasonal foods and fasting.

Cleaning

• *Clean House, Clean Planet* by Karen Logan (Pocket Books) is inspiring. It gives a thousand and one reasons why you shouldn't use conventional cleaners and has alternatives for absolutely everything.

• *Natural Housekeeping* by Beverly Pagram (Gaia) gives old-fashioned household tips and recipes.

Cooking

• *The Bread Book* and *Country Bread*, both by Linda Collister and Anthony Blake (Conran Octopus), are inspiring if you want to get into breadmaking.

• *The Rice Book* by Sri Owen (Doubleday). Alongside bread, rice is a staple food of the world and this book covers absolutely every way of preparing and enjoying it.

• Anything and everything by Jane Grigson (that's not a title of a book, by the way). Her whole hearted enthusiasm for food and cooking is totally inspirational.

General

• *House as a Mirror of Self* by Clare Cooper Marcus (Conari Press) is a wonderful book and essential reading for anyone remotely interested in the idea of a more soulful home. Not specifically about kitchens, but you can adapt the ideas for any room in the house.

• *Spirit of the Home* by Jane Alexander (Publisher) Thorsons. This was my original book about bringing spirit and soul into the home and it explains many of the basic concepts, such as feng shui, space clearing, etc. in more detail.
• *Spirit of the Nursery, Spirit of the Bedroom,* and *Spirit of the Living Room* by Jane Alexander (Publisher) Element. are the companion books to this.

Live Well (Element) is my book on the fascinating Indian tradition of ayurveda. It gives guidance on living according to ayurvedic principles—including diet, seasonal eating, and mindfulness.

If you would like to find out more about my other books and work, or simply want to say "hello," do please visit my website **www.smudging.com**

Picture Credits

Abode UK: 51, 59
Anthony Blake Photo Library: 65, 68, 74, 77
Chilworth Communications for County: 38, 48, 50
Cotswold Company: 29 (left)
The Denby Pottery Company: 25 (middle)
Elizabeth Whiting and Associates: 3, 13, 19, 29 (right), 33, 54, 61, 62 (middle), 62 (right)
Fired Earth: 25 (left)
Foodpix.co.uk/Food Features: 78

The Interior Archive/Fritz von der Schulenburg: 6, 82, 88
Red Cover: (Andreas von Einsiedel) 66, 71; (Brian Harrison) 9, 15, 17, 21, 45, 56, 81; (Graham Atkins-Hughes) 53; (Jake Fitzjones) 22; (James Mitchell) 43 (right); (Ken Hayden) vi, 26, 43 (centre), 46, 73; (Robin Matthews) 43 (left); (Trevor Richards) 3
Robert Harding: 25 (right), 31, 62 (left), 63, 85, 87